# UNITED STATES CIVICS
## ARTICLES OF CONFEDERATION FOR KIDS

### CHILDRENS EDITION
### 4TH GRADE SOCIAL STUDIES

In this book, we're going to talk about the Articles of Confederation. So, let's get right to it!

# WHAT WERE THE ARTICLES OF CONFEDERATION?

The Articles of Confederation was the first document that came up with a plan for the governing body of the thirteen colonies in North America. After over 100 years of British rule, the British colonies in North America decided that they wanted to be free from the British monarchy and have their own government.

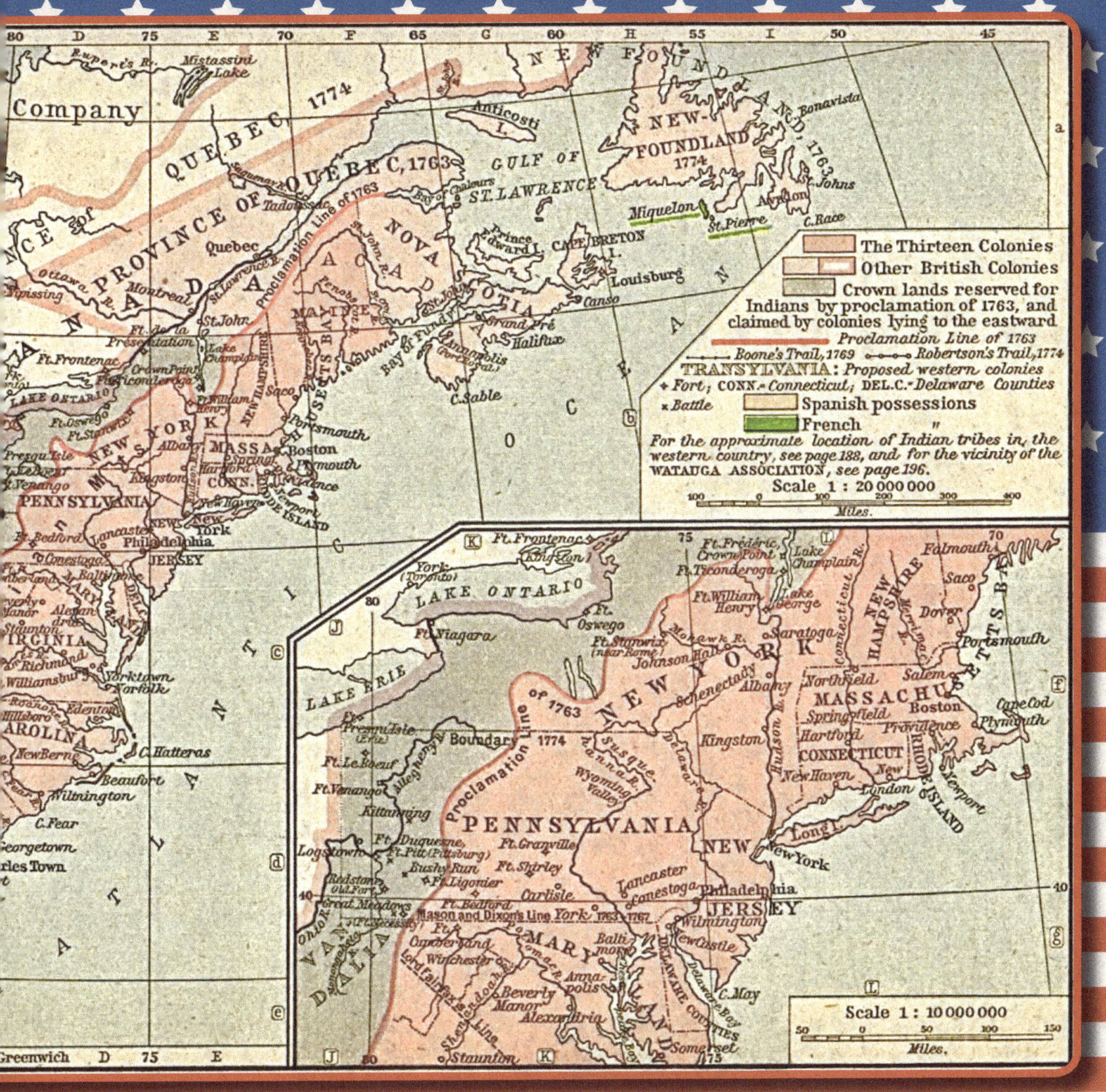
Company
RUPERT'S R.
Mistassini Lake
NEW FOUND
QUEBEC 1774
Anticosti L.
NEW-
FOUNDLAND
1774
Bonavista
N.D. 1763
a
PROVINCE OF QUEBEC, 1763
GULF OF
ST. LAWRENCE
St. Johns
Tadousac
Bay of Chaleurs
NOVA
SCOTIA
Miquelon
St. Pierre
C. Race
Ottawa
Montreal
Quebec
Prince Edward I.
CAPE BRETON I.
The Thirteen Colonies
Nipissing
St. Lawrence
St. John
Grand Pré
Louisburg
Other British Colonies
Ft. Frontenac
Ft. de la Présentation
St. John
Annapolis (Port Royal)
Canso
Crown lands reserved for
Indians by proclamation of 1763, and
claimed by colonies lying to the eastward
LAKE ONTARIO
Ticonderoga
Crown Point
Lake Champlain
Halifax
Bay of Fundy
C. Sable
Proclamation Line of 1763
Ft. Oswego
Ft. Stanwix
Ft. William Henry
Saco
Portsmouth
Boone's Trail, 1769      Robertson's Trail, 1774
Presqu'ile
Le Boeuf
NEW YORK
Albany
Springfield
Boston
TRANSYLVANIA: Proposed western colonies
Fort; CONN.=Connecticut; DEL.C.=Delaware Counties
Venango
Kingston
Hartford
CONN.
New Haven
Plymouth
RHODE ISLAND
Battle      Spanish possessions
PENNSYLVANIA
New York
French
Ft. Bedford
Lancaster
Philadelphia
For the approximate location of Indian tribes in the
western country, see page 188, and for the vicinity of the
WATAUGA ASSOCIATION, see page 196.
Scale 1 : 20 000 000
Conestoga
JERSEY
MARYLAND
DEL.
Miles.
Baltimore
Alexandria
Staunton
VIRGINIA
Richmond
Williamsburg
Yorktown
Norfolk
Edenton
CAROLINA
NewBerne
C. Hatteras
Beaufort
Wilmington
Georgetown
C. Fear
Charles Town
ATLANTIC
Ft. Frontenac
Kingston
Ft. Frédéric, Crown Point
Ft. Ticonderoga
Lake Champlain
Falmouth
York (Toronto)
LAKE ONTARIO
Ft. Oswego
Ft. William Henry
Lake George
NEW HAMPSHIRE
Saco
Dover
Portsmouth
Ft. Niagara
Ft. Stanwix (near Rome)
Johnson Hall
Mohawk R.
Saratoga
Salem
LAKE ERIE
Presqu'ile (Erie)
Boundary 1774
NEW YORK
Schenectady
Albany
Northfield
MASSACHUSETTS
Springfield
Boston
Cape Cod
Ft. Le Boeuf
Proclamation
Susque.
Delaware R.
Hudson R.
Kingston
Hartford
CONNECTICUT
New Haven
Providence
Plymouth
RHODE ISLAND
Newport
Ft. Venango
Wyoming Valley
Kittanning
New London
Long I.
Logstown
Ft. Duquesne
Ft. Pitt (Pittsburg)
Bushy Run
Ft. Granville
Ft. Shirley
PENNSYLVANIA
Lancaster
Conestoga
NEW York
NEW JERSEY
Philadelphia
Redstone Old Fort
Ft. Ligonier
Carlisle
York 1763-1767
Wilmington
New Castle
Great Meadows (Ft. Necessity)
Mason and Dixon's Line
DELAWARE counties
VANDALIA
Ft. Bedford
Cumberland
Lord Fairfax's Line
MARYLAND
Baltimore
Annapolis
DELAWARE BAY
C. May
Winchester
Beverly Manor
Alexandria
Somerset
Shenandoah
Staunton
Scale 1 : 10 000 000
Miles.
Greenwich

AMERICAN REVOLUTIONARY WAR

During the time that the Revolutionary War was being fought, the members of the Continental Congress drafted a document in 1777 that they called the "Articles of Confederation." The goal of the document was to have the thirteen colonies work as a unified country. Although they were not yet an independent country, they needed to begin to work together to put a new government into place.

# WHY DID THE REPRESENTATIVES OF THE COLONIES DRAFT THE ARTICLES OF CONFEDERATION?

Even though they were in the process of getting away from the government of Great Britain, the colonies realized that they would need a new form of government. They wanted to have written guidelines that all the representatives could agree on. It was necessary for the new Congress to be able to organize an army for defense, establish laws for the land, and print forms of money.

Drafting the Articles of Confederation
York Town, Pennsylvania 1777
13c USA

JOHN DICKINSON

# WHO AUTHORED THE ARTICLES OF CONFEDERATION?

John Dickinson was the writer of the initial draft of the Articles of Confederation along with a committee made up of thirteen representatives, one from each colony.

# WHEN DID THE ARTICLES OF CONFEDERATION GO INTO EFFECT?

After the Articles of Confederation were drafted, all thirteen colonies had to approve the document. This process took some time. The first colony to approve it was Virginia in 1777 and the last was Maryland in 1781. The states and the legislative branch had all the power in the new government. There was no executive branch and there wasn't much of a judiciary branch either.

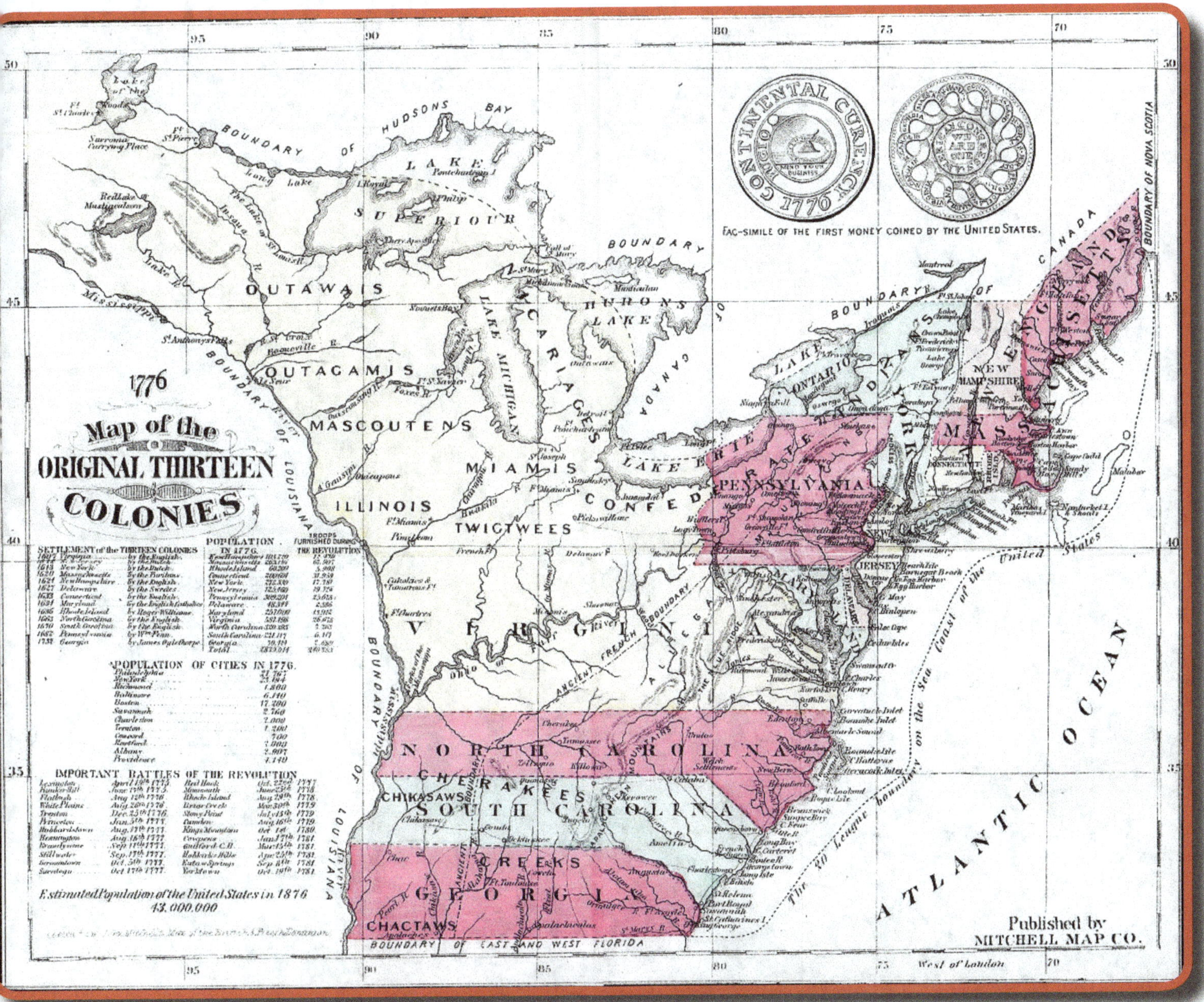


MAP OF THE THIRTEEN ORIGINAL COLONIES

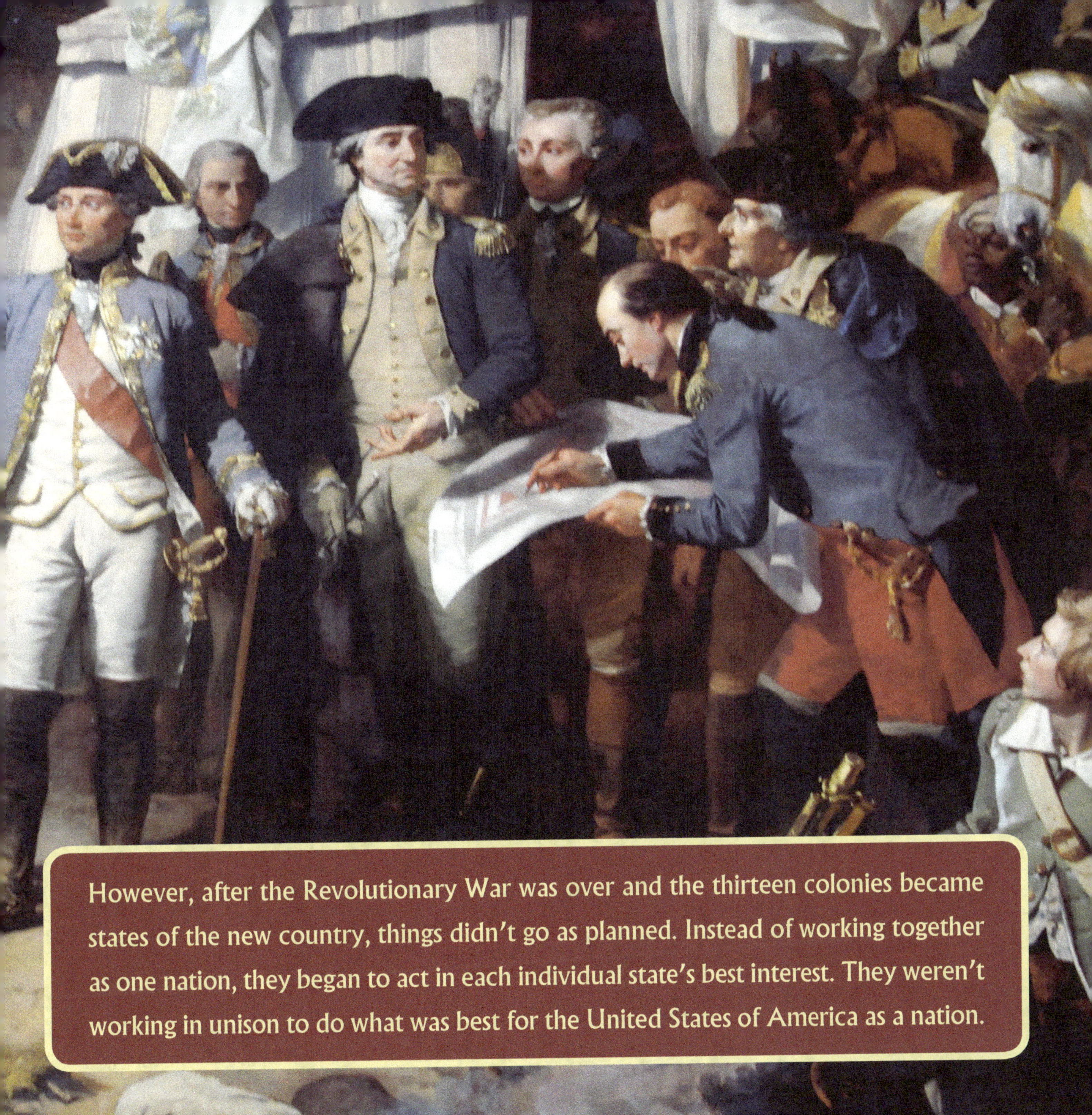

However, after the Revolutionary War was over and the thirteen colonies became states of the new country, things didn't go as planned. Instead of working together as one nation, they began to act in each individual state's best interest. They weren't working in unison to do what was best for the United States of America as a nation.

It became clear that the Articles of Confederation were a good start, but they didn't create the strong government that the United States needed to survive as a country. Another convention was arranged and in May of 1787, the representatives decided to draft a completely new Constitution for the United States.

# THE THIRTEEN ARTICLES

The Thirteen Articles are written in the formal language used at the time. Here is a brief summary of what each article entailed.

## ARTICLE 1

The name of the new country was established as the "United States of America."

# ARTICLE 2

The individual states still had their own governing documents and their powers weren't specifically listed in the Articles of Confederation.

# ARTICLE 3

The union of the states was to be considered a "friendship league" where the welfare of each state was of primary importance. If necessary, they would unite to defend each other from attacks by other countries.

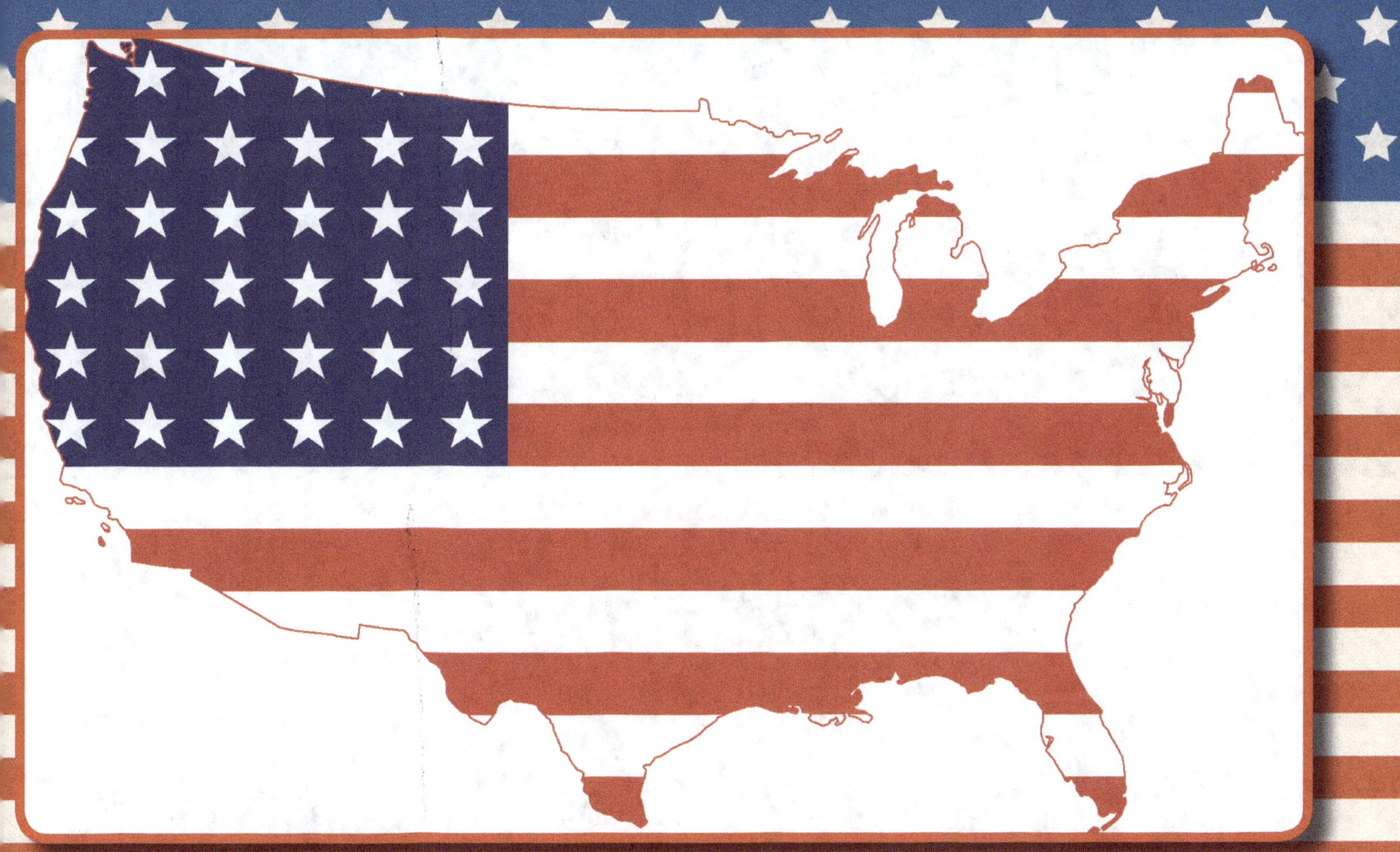

# ARTICLE 4

Citizens were allowed to move freely between the states. However, if someone was a criminal he or she would have to go back to the state where a crime was committed in order to be tried by a jury in a court of law.

# ARTICLE 5

This article established the workings of the Congress. Each state was given one vote and was allowed to send 2 to 7 representatives as their delegates.

# ARTICLE 6

The central governing body would be responsible for negotiations with foreign countries. This might include trade contracts or a declaration of war. Also, the states were allowed to rally citizens to bear firearms in case of an emergency, but they were not allowed to have a professional army.

# ARTICLE 7

The states were given the power to specify ranks in the military, beginning with the highest rank of colonel as well as lower ranks.

# ARTICLE 8

The legislatures of each state would be responsible for raising money to be used in supporting the central or federal government.

# ARTICLE 9

This article gave Congress the power to settle any agreements arising between two or more states. Congress was also given specific powers to communicate with foreign countries for treaties, whether they were for peace, for war, or for importing and exporting. Congress was also tasked with coming up for a plan for standard weights and standard measures.

# ARTICLE 10

A group was founded to act on the behalf of Congress, when it was not in session. This group was described as the "Committee of the States."

# ARTICLE 11

This article established that the country of Canada could become part of the United States if they wished to do so.

# ARTICLE 12

This article stated that debts incurred during the war would be paid off.

# ARTICLE 13

This article explained that the Articles of Confederation would stay in effect until the Congress and all thirteen states agreed to change it or replace it.

EQUAL JUSTICE UNDER LAW

# WEAKNESSES OF THE ARTICLES OF CONFEDERATION

The Articles of Confederation gave the new nation its start, but there were several weaknesses in its coverage, which were later corrected in the United States Constitution that replaced it.

- The Congress didn't have any power to raise taxes. The colonies had just started a war with Great Britain over taxation so it wasn't surprising that they didn't have a plan for how to collect tax.
- There was no system in place for enforcing the laws that Congress passed.
- There was no process for how someone should be tried in a national court.
- Despite their population or geographic size, each colony only had one vote.

In 1788, the Articles of Confederation were left in the past and the new United States Constitution was put into effect. The US Constitution and its subsequent amendments was a much stronger document.

# TIMELINE OF THE ARTICLES OF CONFEDERATION

## THE ARTICLES OF CONFEDERATION ARE CREATED

In November of 1777, the Articles of Confederation are drafted because the colonies needed a system of government. The document kept the federal government in the weaker position and the individual colonies in the position of power. It seemed appropriate at that time since they were in the middle of getting away from the strong British rule.

HENRY MARCHANT, SIGNER OF THE ARTICLES OF CONFEDERATION

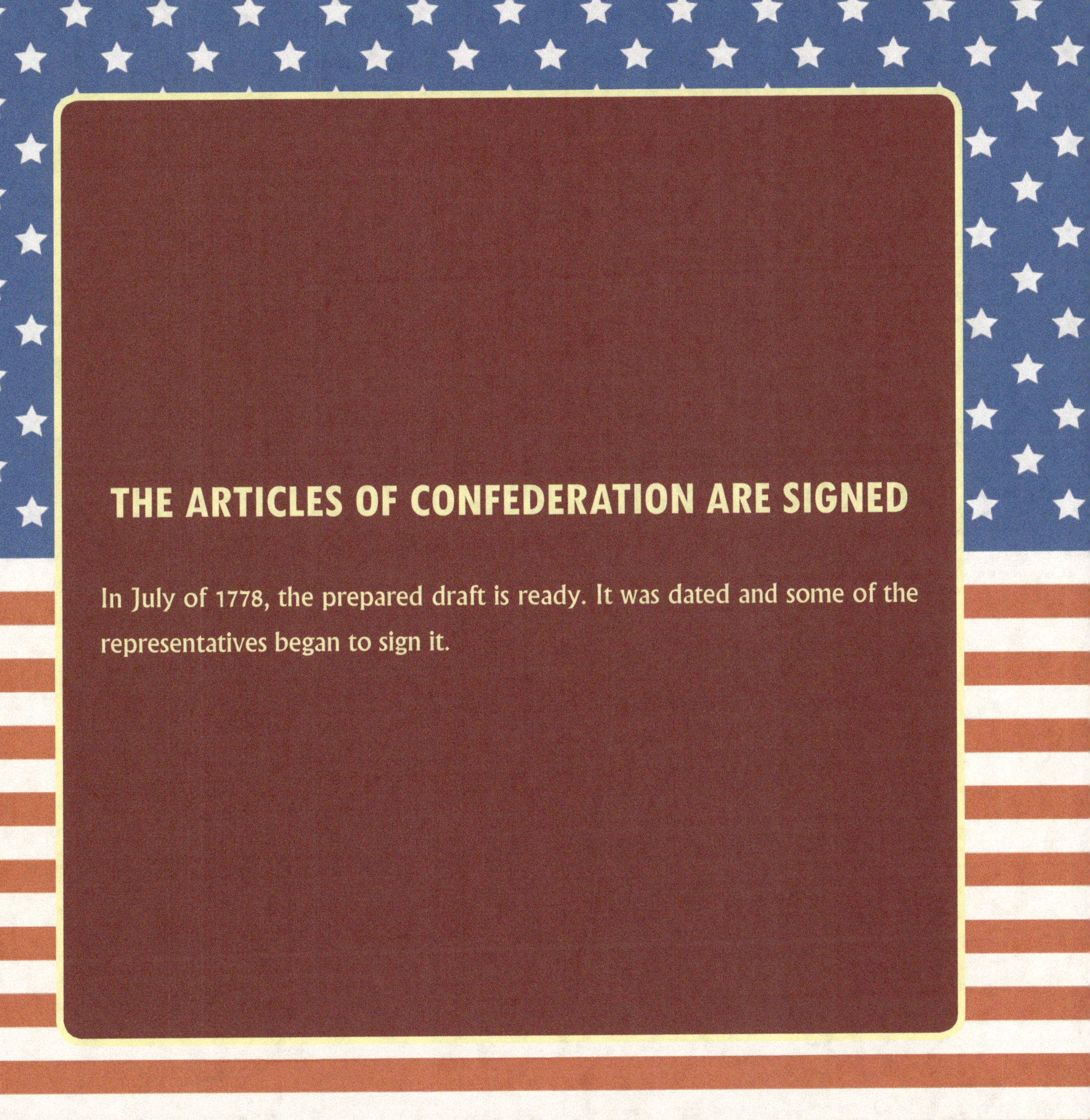

# THE ARTICLES OF CONFEDERATION ARE SIGNED

In July of 1778, the prepared draft is ready. It was dated and some of the representatives began to sign it.

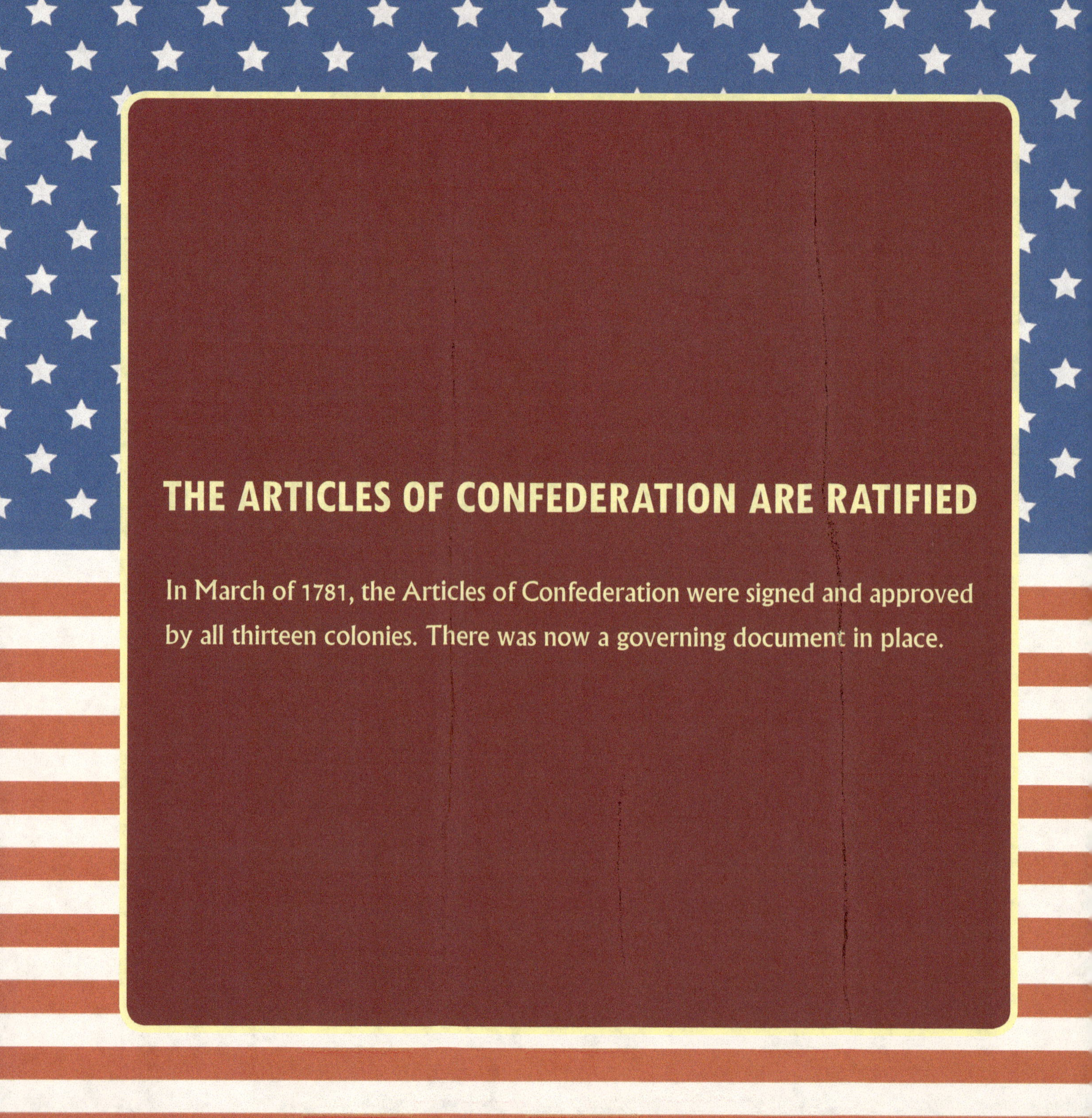

# THE ARTICLES OF CONFEDERATION ARE RATIFIED

In March of 1781, the Articles of Confederation were signed and approved by all thirteen colonies. There was now a governing document in place.

Canada
Nouvelle-Ecosse
Grands
Lacs
New Hampshire
New York
Massachusetts
1
Rhode Island
Connecticut
2
New Jersey
Pennsylvanie
Delaware
Territoires
indiens
Maryland
3
4
Virginie
Appalaches
Caroline du
Nord
Louisiane
Caroline du
Sud
Mississipi
5
Océan
Georgie
Atlantique
Floride
Golfe
du
Mexique
MAP OF THIRTEEN COLONIES

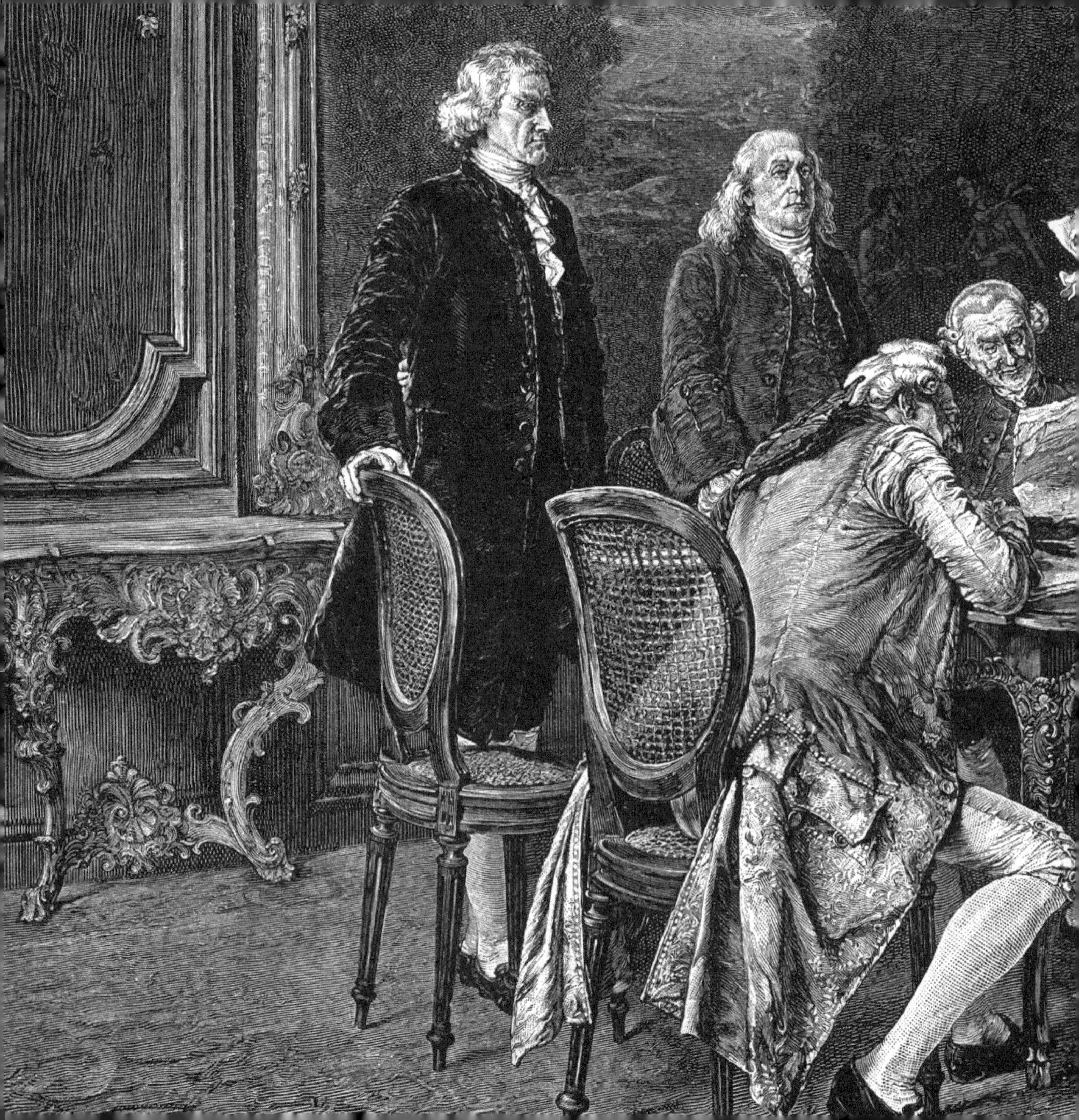

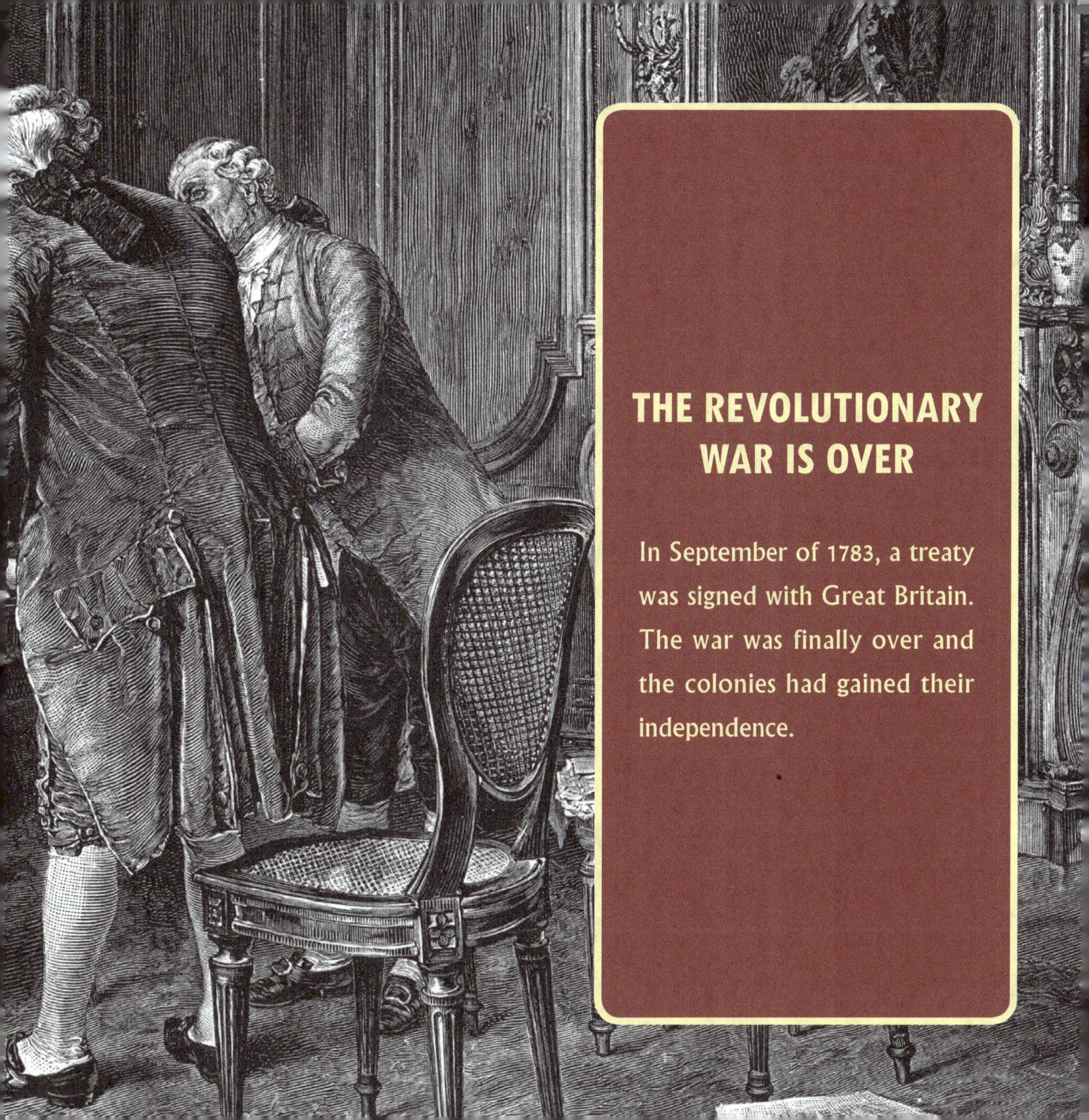


THE REVOLUTIONARY
WAR IS OVER

In September of 1783, a treaty
was signed with Great Britain.
The war was finally over and
the colonies had gained their
independence.

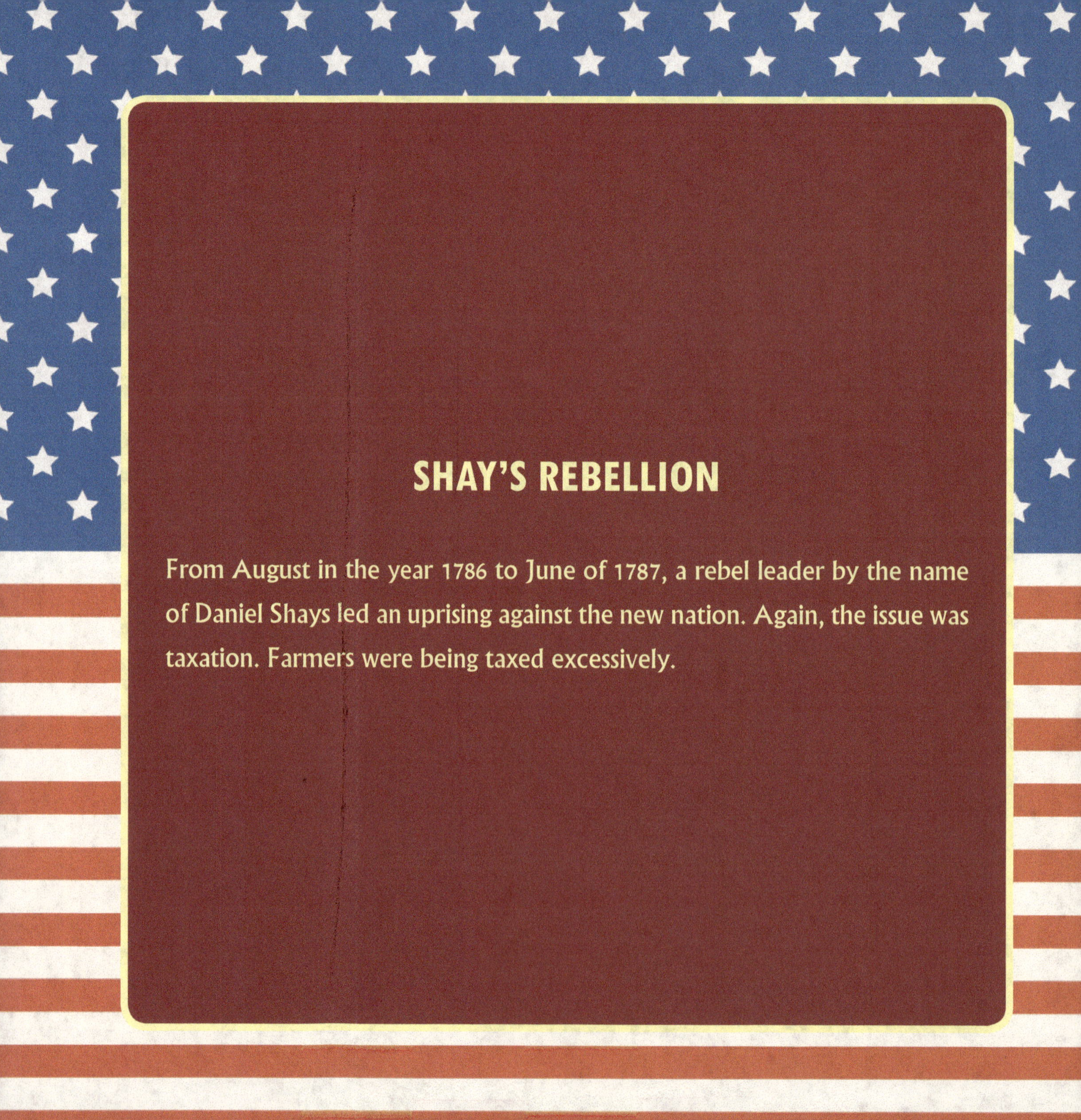

# SHAY'S REBELLION

From August in the year 1786 to June of 1787, a rebel leader by the name of Daniel Shays led an uprising against the new nation. Again, the issue was taxation. Farmers were being taxed excessively.

CAPT. DANIEL SHAYS
1747 — 1825
REVOLUTIONARY WAR
5TH MASS. REGIMENT
BUNKER HILL
TICONDEROGA
SARATOGA
STONY POINT

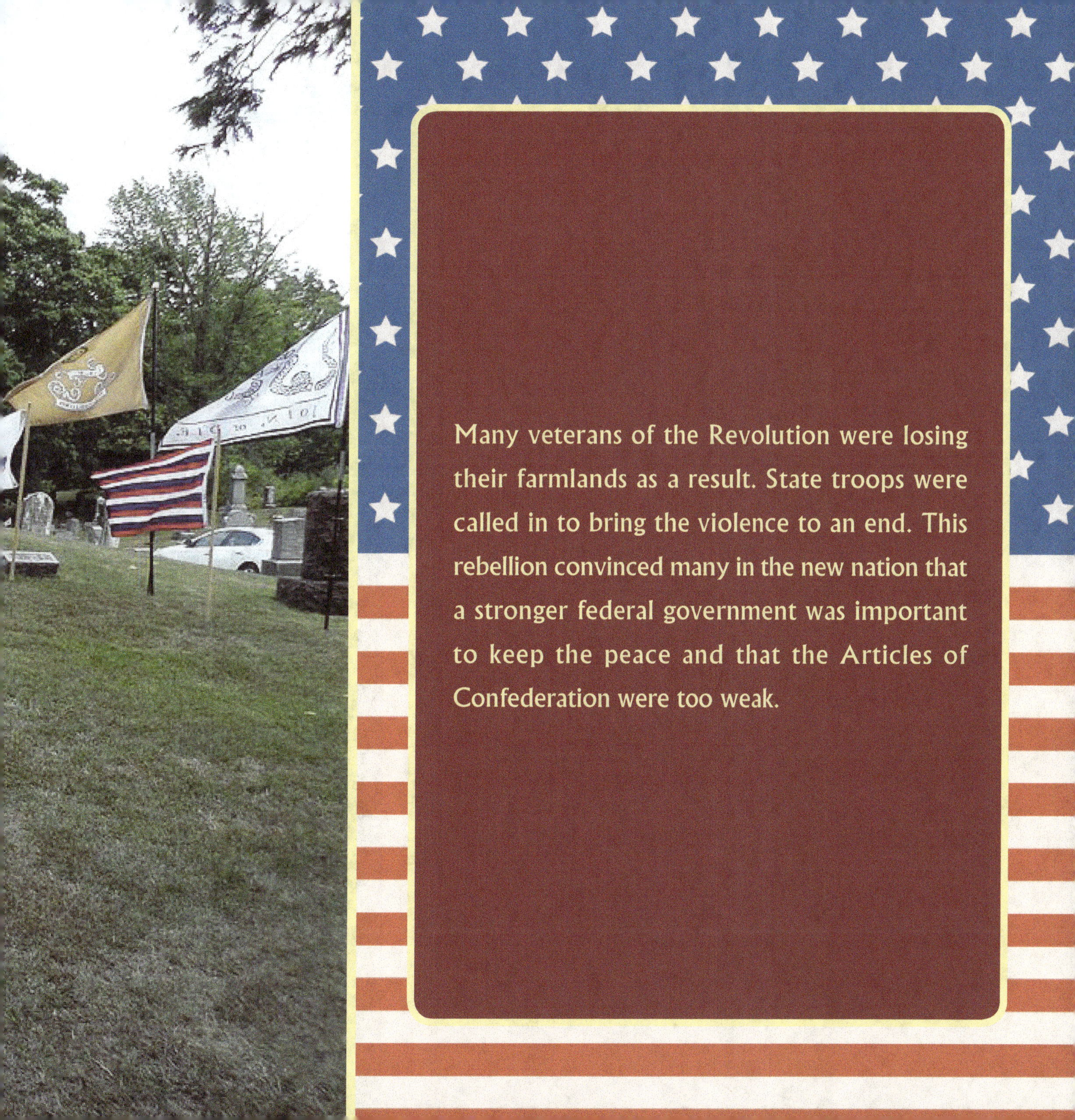

Many veterans of the Revolution were losing their farmlands as a result. State troops were called in to bring the violence to an end. This rebellion convinced many in the new nation that a stronger federal government was important to keep the peace and that the Articles of Confederation were too weak.

# THE ANNAPOLIS CONVENTION

In 1786, at the state of Virginia's request, a meeting was convened to discuss improvements to the government. However, not enough delegates showed up so the meeting would have to be convened again.

ANNAPOLIS

THE CONSTITUTIONAL CONVENTION IN PHILADELPHIA

In May of 1787, there was a convention begun at Independence Hall in the state of Philadelphia. The purpose was to discuss revising the Articles of Confederation to make them stronger. The plan was eventually changed when it was decided that a completely new document was needed.

INDEPENDENCE HALL

# THE US CONSTITUTION IS WRITTEN AND SIGNED

In September of 1787, a new constitution is drafted and discussed in a final session. Thirty-eight out of the forty-one representatives who are present, sign the new US Constitution.

There were still some negotiations needed between those members who wanted a very strong central government and those who wanted the states to have most of the power.

THE ADOPTION OF THE U.S. CONSTITUTION

INDEPENDENCE HALL

# THE US CONSTITUTION IS RATIFIED

One year later in September of 1788, the new United States Constitution is ratified.

# THE US CONSTITUTION BECOMES THE OFFICIAL GOVERNING DOCUMENT

In March of 1789, the new Constitution goes into effect and the Articles of Confederation are no longer used.

# SUMMARY

During the Revolutionary War the Continental Congress drafted a document with thirteen articles. The goal of the document was to provide guidelines for how the union of the thirteen colonies should govern themselves while breaking away from Great Britain. Eventually, all thirteen colonies ratified the document and for a period of years it was the only governing document they had. However, in the long run, the document was weaker than it needed to be to ensure the survival of the United States of America. In 1788, it was abandoned for the stronger document, the United States Constitution.

Awesome! Now that you've read about the
Articles of Confederation, you may want to
read about the United States Constitution
in the Baby Professor book United States
Civics - The US Constitution for Kids | 1787 -
2016 with Amendments.

Visit

BABY PROFESSOR
EDUCATION KIDS

www.BabyProfessorBooks.com

to download Free Baby Professor eBooks
and view our catalog of new and exciting
Children's Books

9 798886 943704